To all my little brown girls who are trying to understand their feelings...

This is just for you!

This journal belongs to:

____

HAPPY

Something made me smile!

I Feel Happy When...

SAD

Something made me
want to cry.

I Feel Sad When...

DISAPPOINTED

I was looking forward to something but it didn't happen.

I Feel Disappointed When...

EXCITED

I can't wait for
something to happen!

I Feel Excited When...

EMBARRASSED

I can't believe
I just did that.
Is everyone laughing
at me?

I Feel Embarrassed When...

CONFUSED

I don't know what is
going on.

I Feel Confused When...

SHY

I just want to hide.

I Feel Shy When...

Amused

That was really funny.

I Feel Amused When...

ANGRY

I'm so mad! I can't believe that happened!

I Feel Angry When...

PROUD

I did a great job!

I Feel Proud When...

ALONE

I feel like I have
no one to talk to.

I Feel Alone When...

NERVOUS

I'm worried about what might happen.

I Feel Nervous When...

SCARED

I'm afraid of what is
happening or what is going
to happen.

I Feel Scared When...

LOVED

I know people love me.
I love me too!

I Feel Loved When...

CONFIDENT

I know that I can do this!

I Feel Confident When...

JOY

I'm so happy!
I don't know if I could be
happier than this.

I Feel Joy When...

SURPRISED

I didn't think that
was going to happen.

I Feel Surprised When...

DETERMINED

I have to do this!

I Feel Determined When...

It's a Good Day When...

It's a Bad Day When...

When I am sad, I cheer myself up by...

When I am angry, I calm down by...

I WILL BE OKAY

NO MATTER WHAT!

The End

(of the book)

The Beginning

(of your emotional journey)

About the Author

Daughter. Dentist. Educator.
Promoter of peace.
Ambassador of ambition. Soldier
of self-love. Former little brown
girl who struggled to find her
magic.

-JLC

www.ingramcontent.com/pod-product-compliance
Lightning Source LLC
Chambersburg PA
CBHW040140240726
48664CB00002B/555